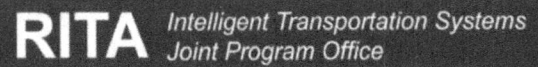

I0427913

ITS Professional Capacity Building:

Setting Strategic Direction 2010-2014

www.its.dot.gov/index.htm
Final Report — March 2011
FHWA-JPO-11-078

U.S. Department of Transportation

Research and Innovative Technology Administration

Produced by Mac Lister
ITS Joint Program Office
Research and Innovative Technology Administration
U.S. Department of Transportation

1. Report No. FHWA-JPO-11-078	2. Government Accession No.	3. Recipient's Catalog No.
4. Title and Subtitle ITS Professional Capacity Building: Setting Strategic Direction 2010-2014		5. Report Date 18 03 2011
		6. Performing Organization Code
7. Author(s) Greer, Elizabeth; Allwell, Cassandra; Burger, Charlotte; Raskin, Larry		8. Performing Organization Report No. N/A
9. Performing Organization Name And Address Noblis / Volpe National Transportation Center 600 Maryland Ave, SW / U.S. Department of Transportation Suite 755 / 55 Broadway Washington, DC 20024 / Cambridge, MA 02142		10. Work Unit No. (TRAIS)
		11. Contract or Grant No. DTFH61-05-D-00002
12. Sponsoring Agency Name and Address U.S. Department of Transportation Research and Innovative Technology Administration ITS Joint Program Office 1200 New Jersey Avenue, S.E. Washington, DC 20590		13. Type of Report and Period Covered Final – October 2010 – December 2014
		14. Sponsoring Agency Code

15. Supplementary Notes

16. Abstract

This document describes the strategy that the ITS Professional Capacity Building (PCB) Program is pursuing to create a 21st century learning environment and build an ITS professional that leads the world in the innovative use of ITS technologies. The strategic plan presents:

- **Introduction**. Describes how the PCB Program is shifting its strategic approach to better meet customer needs.
- **Vision, Mission, and Values**. States the renewed vision, mission, and core values of the Program.
- **Goals and Objectives**. Descibes the strategic plan for 2010 to 2014. Outlines four strategic goals, sets objectives, states anticipated outcomes.
- **Benefits and Conclusion**. Describes benefits of the renewed strategy, outlines how results will be measured, and summarizes actions to be taken to enact the plan.
- **Appendices**. Details stakeholder engagement process and Implementation Plan.

17. Key Words ITS Professional Capacity Building, ITS professional development, ITS training, ITS continuing education	18. Distribution Statement No restrictions. This document is available to the public through the National Technical Information Service, Springfield, Virginia 22161.		
19. Security Classif. (of this report) Unclassified	20. Security Classif. (of this page) Unclassified	21. No. of Pages 56	22. Price N/A

Form DOT F 1700.7 (8-72)   Reproduction of completed page authorized

Table of Contents

List of Figures

Executive Summary

Building an ITS Profession that Leads the World in Innovative Use of ITS Technologies

Envision: a virtual network where Intelligent Transportation System (ITS) professionals access the latest courses, best practices, technical assistance, and professional development opportunities. Enabled by new web-based interactive learning and mobile technologies, transportation engineers, managers, planners, specialists, and public officials will learn from each other while contributing their knowledge and experiences for the benefit of the whole ITS community.

In this new learning environment:

- A traffic engineer will use interactive role play simulation to learn about new incident management technologies to improve both roadway and responder safety.

- A transit official will get answers to questions on dynamic routing and scheduling operations in real time.

- Program managers, planners, and engineers will learn from each other's experiences in implementing proven ITS solutions such as Commercial Vehicle Information Systems and Networks (CVISN) and lead the deployment of the next generation of ITS technologies.

This 21st century digital learning environment brings together a network of professional development and training opportunities with 24-hour accessibility for students, researchers, practitioners, and decision makers working in the ITS field. Such a network will serve the public good by using the latest in learning technologies to leverage a wide base of knowledge assets to maximize safety, mobility, and environmental performance, with potentially far-reaching benefits for the transportation workforce, public agencies, the ITS industry, US global competitiveness, and the traveling public.

This document describes the strategy that the ITS Professional Capacity Building (PCB) Program is pursuing to create this new learning environment and build an ITS profession that leads the world in the innovative use of ITS technologies. To achieve this vision, the PCB Program plans to shift its approach:

From:	To:
Directly providing training	**Leveraging knowledge assets for maximum impact**
Promoting ITS	**Developing ITS champions**
Employing classroom-based practices	**Connecting customers with information in a 21st century learning environment**
Training in existing technology	**Accelerating adoption of emerging technology**
Offering a collection of courses	**Building the ITS profession through certification**

Figure E-1. The PCB Program's Shift in Strategy

Overview of this Document

This strategic plan presents the following:

- **Introduction**. This section of the document provides background on the PCB Program and how it supports the ITS Strategic Research Program. It presents a picture of the changing landscape of the ITS environment and describes how the PCB Program is shifting its strategic approach to better meet customer needs. A summary of customer needs, obtained from results of the 2010 PCB User Workshop, user web meetings, and university web meeting, is presented.

- **Vision, Mission, and Values**. This section of the document states the vision, mission, and values of the PCB Program, as developed and refined by its leadership team.

- **Strategic Goals and Objectives**. This section of the document describes the strategic plan for the PCB Program from 2010 to 2014. It outlines the four strategic goals for the Program and sets objectives and anticipated outcomes for each goal.

- **Benefits and Conclusion**. This section of the document describes some of the potential benefits of the renewed PCB Program strategy, outlines how results will be measured, and summarizes the actions the Program will take to enact the strategic plan.

- **Appendices**. The appendices provide further detail on the PCB Program's stakeholder engagement process and the Implementation Plan for 2010-2014.

Summary of the Strategic Plan

As outlined above, the PCB Program Strategic Plan consists of its vision to *"develop an ITS profession that leads the world in the innovative use of ITS technologies."* This vision is supported by the four core values of the Program: **collaborative, forward-thinking, customer-focused, and results-driven**.

In the next four years, the Program will focus on the following interrelated goal areas:

- **ITS Professional Development** – Equip current and emerging ITS professionals with the knowledge skills and abilities needed to plan, design, deploy, operate, and maintain ITS technologies.
- **Leadership Outreach** – Develop a network of champions who promote the value of ITS.
- **Knowledge Exchange** – Facilitate the exchange of knowledge and innovative ITS solutions.
- **Technology Transfer** – Accelerate technology transfer to bring ITS research and proven solutions to the user community.

When put into action, the values and goals translate into a strategic approach for Program delivery that seeks to **leverage** knowledge assets through partnerships, **accelerate** the adoption of the ITS technologies, **deliver** learning in the most effective and engaging manner, and continuously **evaluate** the Program for maximum impact on the US DOT goals of safety, mobility, and environmental performance.

Figure E-2 shows how the vision, values, and goals relate to each other.

Vision: To develop an ITS profession that leads the world in innovative use of ITS technologies.

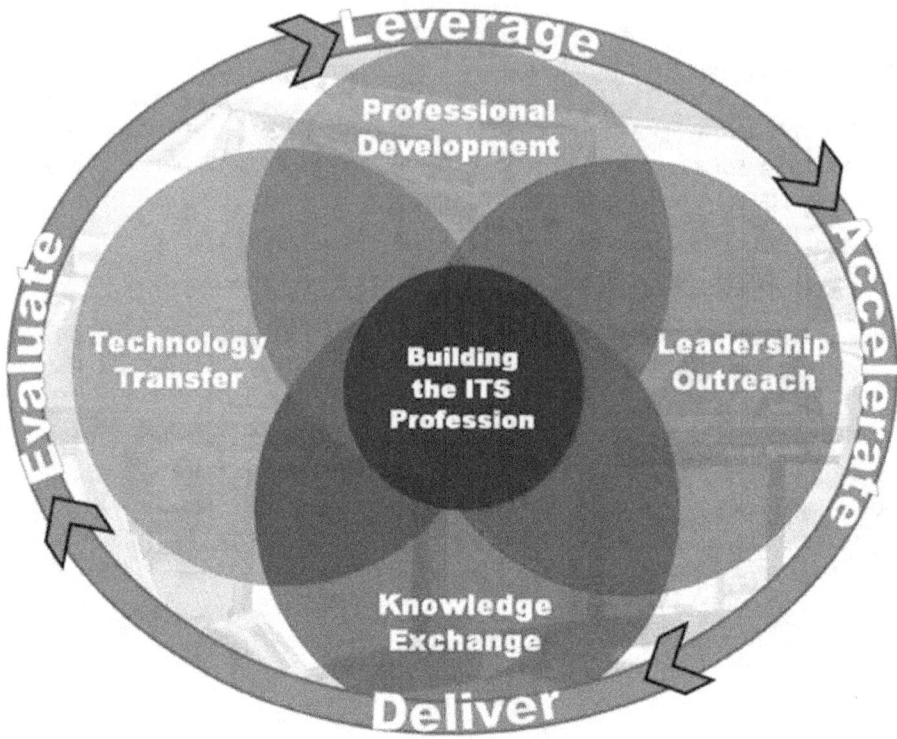

Figure E-2. The ITS PCB Strategic Plan

Chapter 1 Introduction

Since 1996, meeting the challenge of developing the ITS Workforce

The Professional Capacity Building (PCB) Program was launched in 1996 with the recognition that transforming the transportation infrastructure through intelligent transportation systems (ITS) would require a different set of transportation workforce competencies than previously required. The adoption of new technologies, in particular, fast and successful adoption, is highly dependent upon a workforce that is:

- **Aware** of new technologies and research results;
- **Knowledgeable** about procurement and specifications;
- **Skilled** in incorporating new technologies into existing systems;
- **Trained** to oversee the implementation process from a systems perspective; and
- **Capable** of putting ITS technologies into use.

As a cross-cutting program within the ITS Joint Program Office (JPO) of the Research and Innovative Technology Administration (RITA) of the U.S. Department of Transportation, the PCB Program works to ensure the effective implementation and operation of ITS. Since its inception, the Program has successfully advanced knowledge and awareness of ITS through training, technical assistance, and outreach to the ITS practitioner and decision maker.

The ITS Research Program: Transportation Connectivity

For 2010-2014, the ITS JPO has developed a focused research agenda for delivering transportation connectivity through the application of advanced wireless technologies. In this new world, vehicles of all types will 'see' each other and communicate to reduce crashes; motor vehicles will communicate with traffic signals to eliminate unnecessary stops; travelers and commercial carriers will obtain the latest information about routes; and environmentally sustainable modes of transportation will be readily available to the public. At the agency level, transportation and transit managers will use the most current data to assess performance and make decisions on the spot. The entire program is enabled by connectivity between vehicles, the roadway infrastructure, mobile devices, and the agencies charged with keeping it all moving, with the goal of making surface transportation safer, smarter, and greener.

Renewing the ITS Professional Capacity Building Program

The PCB Program is refocusing its agenda to prepare the workforce to adopt these new technologies and to take better advantage of proven ITS solutions. This moment presents an opportunity to reposition the Program to respond to changing user needs, create wider awareness and adoption of ITS technologies, and keep pace with rapid advances in digital technology that are transforming the delivery of learning.

With over 15 years of growth in the ITS knowledge, skills, and abilities of the transportation workforce and ITS now being mainstreamed into transportation operations, now is time for the Program to adopt new strategies to build the ITS profession.

The ITS PCB is moving ...

From:	To:
Directly providing training	Leveraging knowledge assets for maximum impact
Promoting ITS	Developing ITS champions
Employing classroom-based practices	Connecting customers with information in a 21st century learning environment
Training in existing technology	Accelerating adoption of emerging technology
Offering a collection of courses	Building the ITS profession through certification

Figure 1-1. The PCB Program's Shift in Strategy

Defining the Customer

The ITS PCB Program's primary target audience is **the ITS practitioner** from all surface transportation modes - transit, motor carriers (ITS Commercial Vehicle Operations, or ITS/CVO), highways/roadways, and rail. These practitioners work as engineers, managers, planners, and specialists at the federal, state, and local government levels. State and local professionals have direct responsibility for the planning and implementation of ITS in their regions. The federal staff is charged with stewardship responsibilities and oversight authority. Private sector participation in PCB training is encouraged when contractors and consultants are conducting major portions of ITS deployments for public agencies.

As ITS technology continues to evolve and become more mainstream, a broader community of transportation workers from multiple disciplines–roadway designers, public safety, operations and maintenance staff–now require access to ITS learning and professional development.

While building the knowledge and expertise of practitioners is the primary mission of PCB, there is increasing awareness of the role that **decision makers**, such as department managers, public safety officials and elected officials play in adopting and championing ITS technologies. The PCB Program has sponsored awareness activities for this audience, but seeks to expand its impact on this important group of professionals.

Government and university **researchers** are an emerging audience for the ITS PCB Program. As the Program aims to accelerate the adoption of new ITS technologies as envisioned in the ITS Strategic Research program, it will target this group for ITS learning opportunities.

Finally, the PCB Program supports the development of **new ITS professionals**, by providing information about programs of study at U.S. colleges and universities, offering information on careers in ITS, and developing online materials for use in university classrooms.

Meeting New Customer Demands

To better understand current partner and customer needs, the PCB Program conducted a series of workshops in 2010 with key stakeholders, learning providers, and users. Further detail on the findings from these workshops is documented in Appendix B. Overall, several themes emerged from these sessions:

- To better engage existing customers, the Program should provide:

  - **More timely and targeted information**.
  - **Greater access** to content and technical expertise in the ITS Strategic Research program.
  - More **opportunities to learn from experienced professionals** about the lessons they learned from deploying ITS technologies.
  - **Affordable and accessible** courses due to budget and time constraints.
  - Dynamic **social interaction** and **experiential** practice to ground learning.

- To better meet the needs of the future ITS workforce, the program should:

  - **Attract students** to the ITS field and prepare them for the demands of the profession.
  - **Engage leaders** in the transportation field who could become ITS 'champions.'
  - **Engage ITS researchers** in bringing research results into practice faster.

A Catalyst for Knowledge Exchange and Learning

To meet these new demands, the PCB Program plans to shift its approach from direct delivery of courses to working more closely with partners. Universities, professional associations, and modal partners within US DOT will be engaged to grow ITS capacity building for wider impact in a multimodal world. With this new approach, the work of the Program will focus on establishing a core knowledge base for the ITS profession. In the transition period, the PCB Program will continue to provide the curriculum for direct training programs in areas of targeted need. As a result, the PCB Program's role will change to become a catalyst for knowledge exchange and learning—leveraging knowledge assets by connecting user needs with its network of trainers and educators.

Learning from ITS Leaders

In its new role, the PCB Program will facilitate the exchange of knowledge and innovative solutions among experienced policymakers and professionals. This effort will involve outreach to users of proven ITS solutions to develop materials so that decision makers can learn about ITS straight from the source at the peer level.

Using Digital Technology as an Enabler

The PCB Program will take advantage of new web-based and mobile technologies to deliver learning faster and more efficiently. In this 21st century learning environment, users will be better able to assess their own needs and direct their learning toward resources targeted to them, with 24-hour accessibility. The Program will use digital connectivity and emerging social media to promote networking among colleagues wherever they are located, with the aim of accelerating technology transfer and knowledge exchange.

Accelerating Adoption of ITS Technologies

The PCB Program will reach out to the public and private sectors with learning resources aimed at moving the ITS Strategic Research program into deployment. The Program will explore opportunities to engage university researchers in the ITS test beds and other demonstration projects that use hands-on experiential learning techniques.

Building the ITS Profession

As the ITS industry expands, the workforce must evolve as well. The ITS workforce of the future will be: trained in multiple disciplines, with professionals increasingly coming from fields outside transportation engineering; more diverse in age, gender and ethnicity; experienced with multiple modes and applications; and capable of bringing broader systems thinking to complex projects. The PCB Program must adapt to serve this population—from emerging professionals to those nearing the end of their careers. Recognition of ITS as a career through certification is one option being explored to build the profession.

The Challenge of a Changing Workforce

The ITS user community, like the wider U.S. transportation industry, is facing a number of workforce challenges in the coming years. Among these are: an aging workforce, accompanied by anticipated baby boomer retirements; the need to attract and retain a younger and increasingly more diverse workforce; and the need to educate the workforce about emerging technologies that often involve multiple disciplines.

The United States leads the world in the number of science and engineering degrees awarded. In recent years, however, the transportation profession has had a difficult time attracting qualified candidates to federal and state agencies that perform the bulk of transportation operations and maintenance. Transportation projects may not hold the same attraction, and in many cases, do not offer the high salaries available in high technology fields. As global competitiveness and workforce mobility increases, the emerging U.S. ITS industry, like many technology fields, will find itself competing with other countries for knowledge workers.

In the last decade, continuing education opportunities in the ITS field, as in all areas of transportation, have been limited by budgetary and travel restrictions. The complexity of the issues to be addressed and the multiple disciplines involved require a more innovative approach to delivering learning.

The U.S. DOT has made the hiring and retention of a diverse, adaptive, and multidisciplinary workforce a top priority. Continuous lifelong learning, opportunities for knowledge exchange among multiple disciplines and projects, accelerating technology transfer, and building the ITS leaders of tomorrow are key strategies the PCB Program will employ to achieve this strategic imperative. Engaging decision makers in understanding the role an educated workforce plays in adopting ITS solutions is also a critical part of the strategy.

Figure 1-2. The PCB Program's Commitment to Workforce Development

Chapter 2 Vision, Mission, and Values

In support of the ITS Research Program, the ITS PCB Program has established the following vision, mission, and core values.

Vision

> **To develop an ITS profession that leads the world in the innovative use of ITS technologies.**

Envision: A virtual network where ITS professionals access the latest courses, best practices, technical assistance, and career development opportunities, enabled by new web-based interactive learning and mobile technologies, while contributing their knowledge and experiences in ITS for the benefit of the whole community. In this transformed environment:

- An undergraduate or graduate level student learns about professional skills and careers in ITS, researches new Vehicle-to-Vehicle (V2V) and Vehicle-to-Infrastructure (V2I) safety applications for a project, and interacts virtually with experienced ITS professionals about their experience implementing collision avoidance technologies in the field.

- A young professional poses a question about a problem he is experiencing with electronic tolling and gains access to a community of professionals with experience in that area. The young professional reciprocates by sharing an innovative practice he has seen in the field, and contributes a new idea for learning about a particular ITS topic, based on a role-playing game he enjoys in his personal time.

- A mid-career professional managing a project finds web-based, just-in-time courses to provide her team with information they need to complete their current traffic congestion project. While searching, she comes across the Best Practices forum, and takes the opportunity to contribute her most recent ITS project experience. She realizes that many of the forum participants have received leadership training to advance their ITS careers. She enrolls in a professional development course to take her skills to the next level.

- A transportation professional nearing retirement contributes best practice experience through a video log, and poses a series of challenges to the community based upon his long career in ITS. While in semi-retirement, this valued member of the community serves as an advisor and expert in the ITS forums.

- A learning provider who is considering developing an ITS-related course researches what other opportunities are offered in order to avoid duplication. As the course is being developed, the same individual shares online how video case studies are being incorporated to improve learner engagement and asks for participants from the ITS community. A number of ITS practitioners agree to be featured in case studies, a result that serves to raise the profile of their projects and attracts new recruits to the ITS field.

- A decision maker who is considering deploying ITS views model projects to evaluate benefits, costs, and challenges in adopting ITS technologies. From the model projects, the potential sponsor recognizes a peer from another state. The potential sponsor contacts the ITS leader with specific questions about ITS technology and their shared institutional environment. By accessing the ITS PCB knowledge network, the decision maker sees the range of resources available that will ensure successful ITS implementation.

These scenarios highlight the benefits that a more integrated and connected PCB Program can deliver in support of ITS research, deployment, and innovative use. This strategic plan lays out the broad actions that the PCB Program will take in the next four years to achieve this vision. Further details about the specific actions to be taken can be found in the ITS PCB Implementation Plan, in Appendix A of this document.

Mission

"To develop a workforce capable of developing, operating, and maintaining intelligent transportation systems."–SAFETEA-LU, Sec. 5301.

The Professional Capacity Development Program was authorized by Congress in 1996 to develop the workforce competencies necessary to transform the transportation infrastructure through ITS.

Our Customers

The PCB Program serves the ITS workforce, which includes researchers, practitioners, decision makers, and emerging ITS professionals, both in the public and private arenas.

Our Partners

The PCB Program works in partnership with professional associations, universities, and the training programs of U.S. DOT modal administrations to engage the broad technical and organizational expertise needed to provide learning. The PCB Program:

- Works with its partners to determine the knowledge and skills needed for the ITS workforce, and develops the ITS curriculum.
- Provides structured learning directly or through partners in key areas of ITS learning.
- Serves as a clearinghouse for ITS learning opportunities and instructional techniques.
- Facilitates knowledge sharing among researchers, practitioners, and decision makers so that everyone gains from the experience of applying ITS in the real world, and new research results are quickly adopted and put into practice.

Values

As the PCB Program seeks to become the recognized source for learning and knowledge for the ITS professional, we will be:

Collaborative

We seek to *leverage* knowledge and expertise at all modes and stages of ITS technological development. We are open to new ways of thinking about ITS and the learning resources we deliver. We are committed to actively listening to our customers and working with our partners to deliver the best possible program.

Forward Looking

We will promote emerging research in ITS technologies by leveraging new learning techniques to *accelerate* the adoption of ITS. We are open to new ideas and new ways of thinking; we move quickly to take advantage of new technologies and innovative methods of learning.

Customer Focused

We *deliver* programs that are targeted to our customer's needs, whether it be for information about the latest, state-of- the-art ITS technology, or updates on implementing or maintaining established technologies. Our methods of delivery seek to provide the right information to the right audience at the right time. We are as concerned as our customers about managing resources to maximize return on their time and money invested in learning.

Results Driven

We continuously *evaluate* our performance by conducting assessments, actively listening to customers, and adjusting our program so it can be leveraged for maximum results.

Chapter 3 Strategic Goals and Objectives

In consultation with its stakeholders, partners, and customers, the PCB Program leadership has developed four interrelated goals to guide the Program toward achieving the vision of building the ITS profession.

- **ITS Professional Development** – Equip current and emerging ITS professionals with the knowledge skills and abilities needed to plan, design, deploy, operate, and maintain ITS technologies.
- **Leadership Outreach** – Develop a network of champions who promote the value of ITS.
- **Knowledge Exchange** – Facilitate the exchange of knowledge and innovative ITS solutions.
- **Technology Transfer** – Accelerate technology transfer to bring ITS research and proven solutions to the user community.

Each goal is supported by strategic objectives which outline the activities and initiatives the Program will conduct in 2010-2014. The Program developed an Implementation Plan that further identifies the specific actions needed to attain each of the objectives, which is prioritized according to short-term, long-term, and intermediate needs (see Appendix A for details). The Implementation Plan includes measureable outcomes with targets for the next four years. Together, these plans map out a new approach to meeting the needs of existing customers while extending the Program to serve more ITS professionals, with more of the resources needed to do their jobs.

Vision: To develop an ITS profession that leads the world in innovative use of ITS technologies.

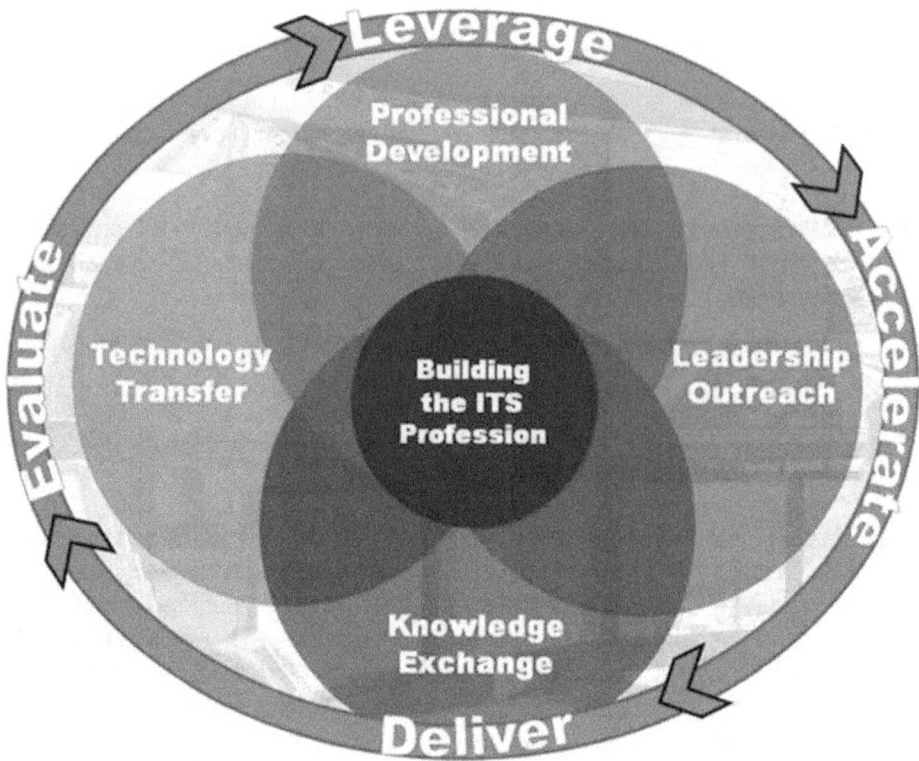

Figure 3-1. The ITS PCB Strategic Plan

Figure 3-1 shows how the four goals work together to achieve the vision of building the ITS profession. The ways of doing business embodied by the Program's core values provide guidance on how to carry out the actions described in the strategic plan.

Goal 1: Professional Development

Equip current and emerging ITS professionals with the knowledge, skills, and abilities to plan, design, deploy, operate, and maintain intelligent transportation systems.

Source: ©iStockphoto.com/track5

Expanding the knowledge, skills, and abilities of the ITS workforce remains an essential part of the PCB Program mission. Users of the Program wish to see continued and strategic use of existing formats such as the Talking Technology and Transportation (T3) webinars, the peer-to-peer (P2P) technical exchange program, and the blended learning instructional courses.

An emerging priority for the program will be to strengthen existing course offerings, while identifying the requirements for competence in ITS, and ultimately promoting certification as an ITS professional. The strategic objectives in Goal 1: Professional Development are:

    1.1. Determine core competencies for the ITS professional.

    1.2. Create a baseline ITS curriculum.

    1.3. Facilitate the incorporation of ITS training into academic programs.

    1.4. Promote an ITS professional certification.

    1.5. Provide ITS continuous learning.

Objective 1.1: Determine core competencies for the ITS professional.

Problem

Users and stakeholders lack consensus about what constitutes the core competencies for ITS. The need for core competencies is underscored by the limited number of universities that offer significant course work or exposure to ITS technologies.

Solution

The PCB Program will work with its partner subcommittees in ITS America, the American Association of State Highway and Transportation Officials (AASHTO), Institute of Transportation Engineers (ITE), and the Transportation Research Board (TRB) to identify the core competencies for ITS professionals so they can be used for staffing, education, and professional development.

The core competencies will represent the minimum set of core knowledge, skills, and abilities needed to begin functioning effectively in the ITS field. They will outline a comprehensive, multidisciplinary, and systematic set of knowledge, skills, and abilities.

Expected Results

Success will be measured initially by progress on a set of core competencies for ITS and the learning objectives for obtaining that competency. Longer term success will be measured by the program's effectiveness in communicating the core competencies and encouraging their adoption by the wider ITS community.

Outputs:

- A catalogue of the core competencies necessary to perform the full range of ITS activities.

- Proposed pathways for training ITS professionals in the specific knowledge and skills required for procuring, deploying, operating, and maintaining ITS technologies.

Outcome:

Core competencies are used by transportation agencies and learning providers to:

- Determine staffing requirements

- Develop job announcements

- Set learning objectives

- Review performance

- Guide career progression

Objective 1.2: Create a baseline ITS curriculum.

Problem

Transportation professionals and managers need to understand what is necessary in order to be proficient in ITS and what course offerings would be best suited for their current needs.

Solution

The PCB Program will develop a baseline curriculum that outlines the learning necessary to become proficient in the ITS field, including the sequence of coursework required to advance to the next level. The curriculum will also specify courses to be taken within tracks in order to become recognized as a knowledgeable professional in a specific ITS technology or other area of expertise. Each component of the baseline curriculum will include the following:

- Learning objectives

- Target audiences

- Description of course materials

- Delivery mechanisms

- Completion requirements

- Evaluation methods

Outputs:

- The components of a baseline ITS curriculum that can be used by partner organizations to design courses according to current models of instructional design.

- A model for evaluation of ITS learning offerings that can be used across the ITS community.

Outcome:

ITS professionals receive the coursework and learning to become proficient in the ITS field.

These components can be used by partner organizations to develop courses or modules according to current models of instructional design.

Expected Results

Success will be measured initially by progress on the development of a baseline curriculum, and in the long-term by the effective design and delivery of learning programs for ITS professionals.

Objective 1.3: Facilitate the incorporation of ITS training into academic programs.

Problem

Academic institutions are challenged to keep pace with educating future transportation professionals about new ITS technologies, as well as adapting their engineering curriculum to provide a multidisciplinary approach required for effective implementation of these solutions.

Solution

The PCB Program will reach out to educators at colleges, universities, and other learning providers to see what resources the Program can provide for use in the classroom and what course materials these organizations can share as online resources. Discovery-based learning, with its emphasis on hands-on activities and public participation in research, offers opportunities to enhance and extend traditional classroom offerings to students and faculty alike.

Ideas being explored include:

- Providing access to professionals from the peer-to-peer program.

- Inviting university researchers to participate in ITS test beds and other hands-on learning opportunities.

- Developing course materials and online curriculum to be provided to faculty.

- Offering better access to information about ITS careers.

- Case studies or pre-designed workshops/projects for student teamwork.

- Sponsoring research grant competitions.

Outputs:

- A plan for engaging universities in developing, delivering, and sharing ITS learning materials.

- Identification of ITS learning materials that can be immediately utilized in the classroom.

- Where gaps exist, produce an ITS curriculum and resources that college and university professors can immediately utilize in the classroom.

Outcome:

The outcome of this initiative is that college and university civil engineering students graduate with sufficient knowledge about ITS to begin working on ITS-related projects at the start of their careers.

Expected Results

Success will be measured by the number of professors using the materials and their effectiveness in the classroom. The program will also track the number of researchers participating in ITS test beds. Working with our university partners, other measures of effectiveness will be developed.

Objective 1.4: Promote an ITS professional certification.

Problem

Transportation professionals choosing to engage in the ITS field need to develop a specialized set of knowledge, skills, and abilities that define the ITS profession. A certified individual will be recognized as having met these specific requirements developed by peers in the profession.

Solution

An ITS certification will recognize the professional stature of individuals working in the field of ITS. There are numerous advantages to developing a supply of qualified professionals to plan, design, deploy, operate, and maintain intelligent transportation systems. These include the ability to measure competence level for the individual and employer, providing a promotion path and means for long-term investment in an ITS career, and increasing the recognition and prominence of the ITS profession.

The PCB Program will act as a catalyst for bringing together professional associations and universities with an interest in ITS professional certification, with the aim of promoting certification.

Expected Results

Success will be measured initially by progress on the development of the professional certification program. Longer term success will be measured by the program's effectiveness in communicating the importance of becoming a certified ITS professional and in how many industry professionals choose to take the exam to enhance their career.

Outputs:

- A white paper outlining issues with certification and recommendations for next steps.

- A preliminary description of the body of knowledge necessary to attain certification as an ITS professional and the requirements for certification.

Outcome:

The initial outcome of this initiative is recognition of ITS as a profession, followed by consensus among the professional associations and universities involved in ITS regarding the core knowledge necessary for a certification in ITS.

Objective 1.5: Provide ITS continuous learning.

Problem

Transportation professionals must operate in a continuous learning environment, constantly striving to improve their professional knowledge and performance. Continuing education activities provide the opportunity to stay current in functional disciplines, new ITS technology, and leadership and management skills. An essential PCB function is to deliver ongoing education about proven and emerging ITS technologies and how to implement them for professionals already working in the field, at all levels of their careers.

Solution

The PCB Program will continue to provide comprehensive, accessible, and flexible ITS learning for the transportation industry. The Program will place the majority of its materials into electronic format for virtual, on-demand, local accessibility. Access to instructors will be provided when hands-on experience and an instructor's presence is determined to be the most appropriate way to provide learning.

In addition, the program will:

- Develop a targeted learning program, focused on priority areas such as ITS standards.

- In partnership with stakeholders such as professional associations, enable state and regional transportation agencies to build their capacity to customize and develop learning programs of their own.

- Take advantage of Web 2.0 technologies to build social contact into course offerings and offer the opportunity to network with fellow ITS professionals.

Outputs:

- Refocused and streamlined delivery of current training resources.

- Revised and updated courses to reflect new ITS developments and emerging topic areas.

- New learning resources to fill identified gaps in knowledge.

Outcome:

The outcome of these program activities is an ITS practitioner who is equipped with the knowledge, skills, and abilities necessary to plan, design, deploy, operate, and maintain ITS applications.

Expected Results

Success of the current program is measured primarily by course evaluations and user satisfaction ratings. As the PCB Program forges new partnerships to broaden its reach and extend ITS learning to more customers, it will evaluate the effectiveness of the new delivery mechanisms and course content.

Goal 2: Leadership Outreach

Develop a network of ITS leaders who promote the value of ITS.

Source: MS PowerPoint

The PCB Program will offer support to decision makers and emerging leaders in ITS who are seeking innovative solutions to the Nation's transportation challenges. Leadership capacity can be developed by building upon the small but passionate network of champions of ITS, and growing this force through networking, mentoring, and coaching. The Program will explore methods of sharing successful ITS implementations including a peer-to-peer network of model users, which can be used to build the capacity of future leaders.

The strategic objectives of Goal 2: Leadership Outreach are:

2.1. Develop a network of ITS champions who promote the value of ITS.

2.2. Highlight best practices and model users.

Objective 2.1: Develop a network of ITS champions who promote the value of ITS.

Problem

A barrier to ITS implementation is that decision makers often lack information about the benefits of ITS and can be reluctant to spend limited resources on what they may consider to be emerging technologies, rather than proven products. These decision makers often learn best from the experiences of their peers, obtained through networking opportunities.

Solution

The PCB Program will identify and document the work of ITS model users, and publicize their contributions to ITS through diverse channels: printed material, video, speaking engagements, and other materials and forums that can be leveraged across geographical areas.

Expected Result

The initiative will produce advocates for ITS who can champion the research program and emerging technologies at professional meetings and in other settings. Sponsors will connect with their peers at the state or local level to further ITS adoption. Success will be measured by the number and diversity of ITS sponsors and their endorsements of ITS solutions.

Outputs:

ITS endorsements via: printed material, video, and speaking roles at professional meetings.

Outcome:

The outcome of this initiative is that decision makers in transportation agencies and other public sector organizations are knowledgeable about the benefits and challenges of ITS, and are motivated to implement ITS solutions.

Objective 2.2: Highlight best practices and model users.

Problem

Twenty years of experience in planning, designing, implementing, operating, and maintaining ITS applications and technologies are now available through the ITS Knowledge Resources databases. These successful solutions need to be shared effectively among all potential user groups. This need is particularly acute among transportation decision makers who need up-to-date information about the benefits and costs of ITS technologies to expedite the ITS investment process.

Solution

This initiative will focus on synthesizing the known benefits and costs of deployed ITS technologies for decision makers. Additional methods of sharing successful ITS implementations among leaders could include: arranging field visits, facilitating just-in-time exchanges with model users, and developing a peer-to-peer network of transportation policymakers.

Outputs:

- Benefits and costs of ITS technologies synthesized for decision makers.

- A database of model users of ITS solutions in the transportation community.

Outcome:

The outcome of this initiative is an expedited decision making process that results in mainstreaming ITS technologies with known benefits.

Expected Results

Success will be measured by:

- The effectiveness of synthesized benefit cost data in making ITS investment.

- The number of agencies seeking best practice solutions from peers that have demonstrated successful ITS solutions.

Goal 3: Knowledge Exchange

Facilitate the exchange of knowledge and innovative solutions among ITS professionals.

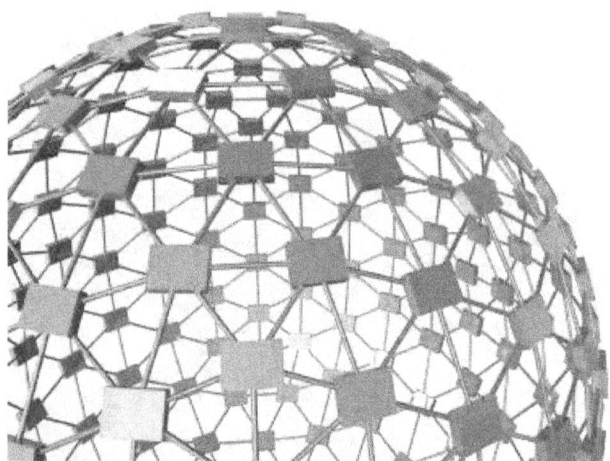

Source: ©iStockphoto.com/alwyncooper

The PCB Program is evolving into a new role as a catalyst for knowledge exchange and learning—leveraging its knowledge assets by connecting user needs with its network of trainers and educators, but also facilitating the exchange of knowledge and innovative solutions among experienced policymakers and professionals. In response to customer needs, the Program intends to draw more on 'real-world experience from the source' in its learning programs.

To achieve Goal 3: Knowledge Exchange, the Program will build a platform for collaborative learning that brings together the full range of ITS learning opportunities while affording opportunities for ITS practitioners as well as its delivery partners to share expertise and best practices.

The strategic objectives of Goal 3: Knowledge Exchange are:

   3.1. Provide an ITS learning portal for one stop shopping of courses, technical assistance, technology transfer, and Peer to Peer (P2P) events.

   3.2. Build a knowledge-sharing community for just-in-time learning among practitioners.

   3.3. Develop a collaborative environment for learning providers to share their expertise.

Objective 3.1: Provide an ITS learning portal for one stop shopping of courses, technical assistance, technology transfer, and Peer to Peer (P2P) events.

Problem

ITS learning assets are spread across multiple locations and organizations. Customers have a strong desire to draw on practitioner knowledge through best practices and peer exchanges, either in-person or online, yet there are limited opportunities to do so. Many users wish to exchange their tacit knowledge and innovative solutions through facilitated sessions, whether via discussion forums or video conferencing. The PCB Program will use technology as an enabler of this intrinsic desire to connect and collaborate.

Outputs:

- Business Case
- Prototype online ITS learning portal
- Live ITS learning portal

Outcome:

The outcome of this initiative is a prototype learning portal that is used by the ITS community for continuous learning and ultimately, more effective ITS deployments.

Solution

The PCB Program will develop an integrated online presence that:

- Provides access to the full range of learning available to the ITS professional from the PCB Program and its modal partners, including such resources as the archived T3 webinars and in the future, video interviews and tutorials.

- Provides a better user experience.

- Allows participants to engage in knowledge exchange and collaboration.

- Collects and incorporates user feedback.

Expected Results

Success will be measured by progress on the development of an ITS learning portal prototype, and its effectiveness once it is launched. Possible measures include meeting target development dates, number of users, and user feedback on the learning portal's usefulness.

Objective 3.2: Build a knowledge-sharing community for just-in-time learning among practitioners.

Problem

Transportation professionals face problems and challenges ranging from important investment decisions to troubleshooting an ITS application or tool. Typical questions faced on a daily basis include:

- *How should a transportation agency choose an ITS solution from a list of high priority capital improvement projects?*

- *What ITS applications should be considered when improving a transportation corridor? What are the benefits and costs of these ITS solutions?*

- *How should a multi-million dollar project be phased? What are the roles and responsibilities of the coalition of transportation agencies?*

In all of these cases, industry practitioners wish to connect with and leverage the real world experiences of other practitioners. They may not have the resources or desire to attend a training class or an association meeting, but they wish to learn from others' direct experiences. Moreover, the issue they are facing may be so immediate that there is no course offered, or they just need a quick response to a troubleshooting question.

Outputs:

- A forum to share experiences, best practices, and lessons learned.
- A user interface relating transportation problems with ITS applications and solutions.

Outcome:

- Better decisions concerning ITS investment, planning, and deployment.
- Greater job satisfaction and lower attrition rates in the profession stemming from pride in sharing knowledge.

Solution

Industry practitioners, specialists, and Subject Matter Experts (SMEs) will share their knowledge, experiences, best practices, and lessons learned with others seeking solutions to transportation challenges. This solution will build upon the existing Knowledge Resource databases, but make them more dynamic and interactive. Information from practitioners could be obtained through an open forum, an "Ask an Expert" function, or as a decision support tool.

Expected Results

Success will be measured by progress on the development of the Knowledge-Sharing Community prototype, its effectiveness once launched, and its continued usefulness as measured by users and contributors. Possible measures include number of users accessing the community, number of responses users receive, timeliness of "expert" responses, and user feedback on the community's usefulness.

Objective 3.3: Develop a collaborative environment for learning providers to share their expertise.

Problem

There are numerous educational offerings and learning providers in the ITS field. Courses are offered by a variety of organizations such as state or local agencies; federal training partners such as Federal Highway Administration (FHWA), National Transit Institute (NTI), and National Highway Institute (NHI); and universities, professional associations, and private sector vendors of ITS technologies.

Learning practitioners in these organizations wish to communicate, share best practices, and coordinate their efforts, where possible, to avoid overlap and offer a consistent curriculum in ITS technologies.

Solution

As new technologies and research findings emerge, it is imperative to accelerate the process of disseminating these results throughout the ITS community. This is the first challenge that the newly formed Learning Collaborative will consider. The first step is to identify leaders in ITS learning who are interested in collaborating, willing to 'seed' content, and build networks of colleagues they can invite to participate. Such an effort will build a culture of collaboration, continuous learning, and rapid deployment of best practices in learning and professional development.

Outputs:

- Learning collaborative charter

- Key features of a learning collaborative virtual environment

- Audit of available learning resources and gaps

- Documented methods to share and disseminate best practices in learning and professional development

Outcome:

The long-range outcome of this initiative is improved and streamlined course offerings, measured by learning provider feedback and student evaluations.

Expected Results

By participating in the learning collaborative, educational providers will:

- Devise methods to rapidly disseminate research and deployment knowledge about ITS, through train-the-trainer and other approaches

- Share innovative techniques for delivering learning

- Develop and share evaluation practices

Success will be measured initially by:

- Number and diversity of learning providers who participate

- Progress toward development of learning collaborative virtual environment

- Assessment of value to learning collaborative members

Goal 4: Technology Transfer

Accelerate technology transfer to bring ITS research and proven solutions to the user community.

Source: ©iStockphoto.com/leungchopan

The ITS PCB Program is moving to accelerate new research and prototypes into market ready technologies that can be adopted by agencies. The Program understands technology transfer as:

Technology transfer encompasses activities leading to the adoption and implementation of new-to-the-user products or procedures by any user or group of users. Technology transfer may involve printed and electronic materials, education and training, knowledge transfer, and technical assistance. Communications options and tools are used to facilitate technology transfer.[1]

This goal uses digital technology as an enabler to bring the most current ITS research and solutions to the ITS user community. Leading edge technological innovations such as social media, mobile application devices, and new learning practices such as interactive games and video will be harnessed to encourage fast and successful adoption of ITS technologies.
The strategic objectives of Goal 4: Technology Transfer are:

    4.1. Increase awareness of current research through pilots and demonstrations that allow interactive hands-on learning.

    4.2. Embed training and outreach into the research and development process to move ITS innovation into the market faster.

---

[1] National Cooperative Highway Research Program, Synthesis 355: Transportation Technology Transfer: Successes, Challenges, and Needs. 2005. At:
http://onlinepubs.trb.org/onlinepubs/nchrp/nchrp_syn_355.pdf.

Objective 4.1: Increase awareness of current research through pilots and demonstrations that allow interactive hands-on learning.

Problem

Emerging and current ITS professionals are not sufficiently aware of or motivated to apply new ITS technologies.

Solution

Provide exposure and build competence in specific ITS technologies through the use of the ITS test beds, pilots, and demonstrations. Use interactive approaches, such as video game simulations, to provide experiential learning in ITS technologies.

Expected Results

The PCB Program expects to develop training on how private sector and educational organizations can participate in the ITS test beds. In the long term, the program hopes to produce interactive tools based upon users' experience with ITS demonstrations and simulations to bring this experience to a wider audience. Success will be measured by the number of professionals participating and the impact the learning has on their motivation and ability to apply ITS solutions.

Outputs:

- Training materials for the use of ITS test beds by private sector and educational organizations.

- Other simulation-based training material.

Outcome:

Practitioner's participation in test beds and other simulation environments provides the experience and motivation to apply ITS solutions, leading to accelerated application of ITS solutions in the field.

Objective 4.2: Embed training and outreach into the research and development process to move ITS innovation into the market faster.

Problem
One of the challenges of accelerating ITS technology adoption is keeping up with the pace of ITS innovation. It can take anywhere from 6 to 12 months to design and test a new course once an ITS prototype is developed. By that time, many ITS technologies are already deployed and some are superseded by new research results.

Solution
This initiative will identify and develop processes and procedures to accelerate ITS research into practice, including:

- **Targeted Audiences**: The new approach will specifically target audiences who will benefit from use of the new technologies, and to deliver a more focused approach on *"Why adopt this technology?"* and *"How do I successfully adopt and use it?"*

- **Faster Adoption**: Plans will be developed with research managers to identify how outreach and professional capacity building can be integrated into the technology development, testing, and evaluation lifecycle.

- **Connectivity and Interoperability:** The growing use of ITS standards and system enterprise architectures offers agencies a means for extending existing systems and faster incorporation of technologies into those systems. The ITS standards and architecture courses will be updated to demonstrate how to leverage these opportunities.

Outputs:
A set of recommendations for a template to be used cooperatively by ITS research managers and PCB staff to plan for technology transfer activities including training and outreach.

Outcome:
Once processes are in place, the outcome is to have outreach and course materials developed on an accelerated schedule to be determined jointly by ITS research managers and the PCB Program.

For proven solutions, the outcome is a greater number of implementations in shorter time frames. Specific implementations will be tracked by the PCB Program.

Expected Results
The result of this initiative is the more timely development of material to assist in ITS technology adoption. The ITS Standards and Architecture courses will be the first subject areas where this new technology transfer process model will be applied. Success will be measured by progress toward the accelerated development of course modules in these subjects.

Chapter 4 Benefits and Conclusion

Benefits

In the transformed environment envisioned by this plan, **transportation professionals,** including engineers, managers, planners, and technical specialists, will access the latest in ITS courses, best practices, technical assistance, and career development opportunities while contributing their knowledge and experiences in ITS for the benefit of the whole community. These professionals will increase their knowledge and expertise so they can effectively plan, procure, and deploy ITS technologies. In addition, they will provide leadership within their organizations on ITS issues and promote the ITS profession.

Universities and learning providers in universities, professional associations, and the training programs of the U.S. Department of Transportation's modal partners will gain the opportunity to collaborate with other learning providers to share effective learning techniques, participate in ITS research through test beds and other pilots, and improve their access to customers.

Transportation agencies will benefit from a workforce that is better trained to implement, operate, and maintain ITS technologies. They will achieve their recruiting and retention goals due to increased on-the-job learning opportunities and pride in the profession. Agencies will gain access to experts and leaders in the ITS field to learn about best practices and innovative solutions in ITS. They will have the opportunity to capitalize on ITS research moving more rapidly into the marketplace.

Industry benefits from the PCB Program's increased emphasis on technology transfer, and its outcome of a workforce that is well positioned to deploy new technology as it emerges from public or private sector research.

There will be benefits to **U.S. competitiveness** deriving from a better educated workforce that can make important contributions to the U.S. economy, by improving the mobility of people, goods, and services through the transportation infrastructure.

The Nation relies upon this well-functioning transportation infrastructure to enable domestic productivity and economic growth. In addition, the growing global market for ITS technologies is estimated at $20 billion with 22.2 percent annual growth over the next five years.[2] The U.S. ITS industry can position itself to take advantage of this growing market by educating the transportation workforce on emerging ITS technologies.

---

[2] "Technologies for Intelligent Transportation Systems, "BCC Research, October 2010 at http://www.reportlinker.com/p0326195/Technologies-for-Intelligent-Transportation-Systems.html.

The ultimate beneficiary is the **traveling public** who will benefit from the expanded knowledge of the ITS workforce in providing travelers with safe, secure, efficient, and environmentally sustainable transportation choices.

Measuring Success

As a results-driven organization, the PCB Program seeks to continually improve its performance. Ultimately, this Strategic Plan will be evaluated for its effectiveness in supporting the ITS Strategic Research vision of:

"A national multi-modal surface transportation system that features a connected transportation environment around vehicles of all types, the infrastructure, and portable devices to serve the public good by leveraging technology to maximize safety, mobility, and environmental performance." [3]

The PCB Program works toward attaining this long-term outcome of more successful, cost effective deployment of ITS technology. However, since multiple factors determine the outcome of a deployment, it can be challenging to measure the effect of a particular course or the overall capacity building effort on a specific implementation. To meet this challenge, the Program will develop assessments that measure short term learning outcomes, intermediate actions, and long-term impacts that lead to successful adoption of ITS to maximize safety, mobility, and environmental performance.

The Implementation Plan assigns a measurable outcome and target to each of the strategic objectives in support of the four major Professional Capacity Building goals. The annual adoption, refinement, and monitoring of these measures is imperative to the success of the overall strategy. The PCB Program will put in place an assessment process for monitoring annual progress toward these strategic objectives.

The PCB Program views strategic planning as an ongoing process carried out in consultation with its partners and stakeholders. The Program will continue to conduct outreach and solicit feedback on the Plan through the PCB Program website and professional meetings and adjust its strategy to meet new customer demands and changing circumstances.

Conclusion

The ITS Professional Capacity Building Program is committed to developing the workforce needed to transform America's transportation infrastructure into a multimodal system that provides travelers and businesses with safe, secure, efficient, and environmentally sustainable transportation choices.

In the next four years, the PCB Program will begin educating transportation professionals about exciting new technologies emerging from the ITS Strategic Research program. Now is the time to take advantage of new developments in learning delivery to engage ITS researchers, practitioners,

---

[3] US DOT, Research and Innovative Technology Administration. ITS Strategic Research Plan, 2010-2014, 2010. http://www.its.dot.gov/strat_plan/index.htm.

decision makers, and emerging professionals in exchanging knowledge about proven solutions and developing the innovative ideas of the future. By implementing its strategic goals of continuous lifelong learning, providing opportunities for knowledge exchange among multiple disciplines and projects, accelerating technology transfer, and building the ITS leaders of tomorrow, the PCB Program will achieve its vision of developing an ITS profession that leads the world in innovative use of ITS technologies.

Appendix A Implementation Plan

Moving from Strategy to Action

Successful execution of the PCB Program strategy requires initiatives to move the Program from its current state to the desired future state. The PCB Program staff developed action plans for each of the 12 objectives within the four goals of the strategic plan, using the following criteria as guidance for selection and prioritization:

The actions in support of the objectives should:

- Maximize impact of vision and mission;
- Focus on a mix of short-term gains and long-term achievements;
- Make effective use of existing resources while including some high priority initiatives that may require additional resources; and
- Contain expected outcomes to answer the question, *"How will we know when we attain the objective?"*

Enacting the Implementation Plan will require close collaboration with PCB Program stakeholders and partners. While understanding the evolving nature of the Plan, these action plans are the first step in determining mutually agreed upon actions, timeframes, performance measures, and targets to achieve the desired outcomes of the PCB Strategic Plan.

Table A-1 provides a summary of the objectives with the estimated timeframe for achieving them. Some activities identified in the Action Plan are ongoing through FY 2014.

- **Short-term** – objectives are complete within one year, by the end of FY 2011;
- **Intermediate-term** – objectives are complete within one to three years, by the end of FY 2013; and
- **Long-term** – objectives are complete within one to four years, by the end of FY 2014.

Table A-1. Timeframe for Achieving PCB Objectives

Goal	Objective	Timeframe		
		Short-term	Intermediate-Term	Long-term
Professional Development	1.1 Determine Core Competencies			
	1.2 Create Baseline ITS Curriculum			
	1.3 Facilitate the Incorporation of ITS Training into Academic Programs			
	1.4 Promote an ITS Professional Certification			
	1.5 Provide ITS Continuous Learning			
Leadership Outreach	2.1 Develop a Network of ITS Champions			
	2.2 Highlight Best Practices and Model Users			
Knowledge Exchange	3.1 Provide an ITS Learning Portal			
	3.2 Build a Knowledge Sharing Network for Just-in-Time Learning			
	3.3 Develop a Collaborative Environment of Learning Providers			
Technology Transfer	4.1 Increase Awareness of Current Research through Pilots and Demonstrations			
	4.2 Embed Training and Outreach into the Research and Development Process			

Crosscutting Activities

In addition to the objectives and associated actions outlined in this Implementation Plan, there are several crosscutting program activities associated with the ITS PCB Program, including evaluation, stakeholder outreach, and general management.

Evaluation

The adoption, refinement, and monitoring of performance measures is imperative to the success of the overall strategy. The ITS PCB Program is committed to evaluating each of its goals and objectives, and when necessary, modifying activities to ensure success.

Outreach

Effective information dissemination about the products and services of the Program are critical to its success. Activities may include brochures, websites, and presentations at meetings.

Management

The PCB Program will carry out effective program management to ensure that tasks are performed within scope and budget.

Action Plans

Each of the 12 action plans below presents an objective, its associated goal, background information, activities to achieve the objective, and the intended outcomes. The tables include performance measures, performance targets, and timeframes for completing the objective. The performance measures and targets are still evolving, and in many cases need to be determined in concert with the partner delivering the learning resources outlined in the action plans.

Objective 1.1: Determine Core Competencies	
Goal 1: Develop the ITS Profession	
Background: The PCB Program will work with its partner organizations in ITS America, the American Association of State Highway and Transportation Officials (AASHTO), Institute of Transportation Engineers (ITE), and the Transportation Research Board (TRB) to identify the core competencies for ITS professionals so they can be used for staffing, education, and professional development.	
Actions: 1. Develop analysis of core competencies. 2. Coordinate with internal U.S. DOT workforce development efforts. 3. Conduct outreach. 4. Validate findings.	
Outcomes: Core competencies are used by transportation agencies and learning providers to: • Determine staffing requirements. • Develop job announcements. • Set learning objectives. • Review performance. • Guide career progression.	
Measures: • Acceptance/adoption of the ITS PCB Program core competencies • Number of agencies using ITS core competencies in hiring practices • Percent of state DOTs that integrate ITS PCB core competencies into hiring or training practices	**Target:** • 100 percent ITS America, AASHTO, ITE, and TRB • 50 percent annual increase • 40 percent by 2014
Timeframe: Short-term – Actions 1-2 Intermediate-term – Action 3 Long-term – Action 4	

Objective 1.2: Create a Baseline ITS Curriculum

Goal 1: Develop the ITS Profession

Background:

The PCB Program will develop a baseline curriculum that outlines the learning necessary to become proficient in the ITS field, including the sequence of coursework required to advance to the next level. The curriculum will also specify courses to be taken within tracks to become recognized as knowledgeable in a specific ITS technology or other area of expertise.

Actions:

1. **Develop inventory of current ITS courses.**
2. Map to core competencies.
3. Develop gap analysis.
4. Update curriculum based upon gap analysis.

Outcomes:

- ITS professionals are proficient in the ITS field after participating in recommend coursework sequence .

Measures:	Target:
• Completed assessment of a baseline ITS curriculum • Number of learning programs for ITS professionals using the baseline ITS curriculum in the design and delivery of training or programming	• Full assessment complete by end of 2011 • 50 percent annual increase

Timeframe:

Short-term – Action 1
Intermediate-term – Actions 2-3

Objective 1.3: Facilitate the Incorporation of ITS Training into Academic Programs

Goal 1: ITS Professional Development

Background:

The PCB Program will reach out to educators at colleges and universities to provide learning materials about new ITS technologies, while obtaining course materials from these learning providers to share online. The Program will present a UTC Workshop with the aim of locating a partner for a pilot online course materials and curriculum.

Actions:

1. **Interview university stakeholders to better understand needs and gaps.**
2. Create university strategy.
3. Present PCB-focused UTC workshop.
4. Develop partnership with university to define pilot effort.
5. Identify university training material.
6. Develop university training material.

Outcomes:

- College and university engineering students graduate with sufficient knowledge about ITS to begin working in the profession at the start of their career.
- College and university engineering students develop knowledge, skills, and abilities in identified ITS competencies.
- Pilot University Training Material meets ITS learning objectives outlined for recent graduates in the field.

Measures:	Target:
- Number of civil engineering graduates pursuing career in ITS - Assessment of Student KSAs (determined by course instructor) - Percent of training material meeting PCB criteria	- 50 percent annual increase - 90 percent of students receiving university training material meet KSAs - 90 percent by 2014

Timeframe:

Short-term – Actions 1-2
Intermediate- term – Action 3
Long-term – Actions 4-6

Objective 1.4: Promote an ITS Professional Certification

Goal 1: ITS Professional Development

Background:

The PCB Program will act as a catalyst for bringing together the professional associations and universities with an interest in ITS professional certification, with the aim of promoting certification.

Actions:

1. **Write White Paper outlining issues with certification and recommendations for next steps.**
2. Present White Paper findings.
3. Develop approach for certification program.
4. Implement certification program.

Outcomes:

- Recognition of ITS as a profession.
- Consensus among the professional associations and universities involved in ITS regarding the core knowledge necessary for a certification in ITS.

Measures:	Target:
• Number of academic programs that cover ITS certification	• 50 percent annual increase
• Number of certified ITS professionals	• 20 percent annual increase after certification is offered
• Number of agencies requiring or preferring ITS certification	• 20 percent annual increase

Timeframe:

Short-term – Actions 1-2
Intermediate-term – Action 3
Long-term – Action 4

Objective 1.5: Provide ITS Continuous Learning

Goal 1: Develop the ITS Profession

Background:

The PCB Program will provide ongoing comprehensive, accessible, and flexible ITS learning to the transportation industry. The Program will place the majority of its materials into electronic format for virtual, on-demand local access bility. Instructor led learning will be provided in conjunction with professional meetings to maximize customer's return on travel and training investments. Revised and updated courses will be offered to reflect ITS developments, and new courses will be developed in emerging topic areas.

Actions:

1. **Develop new courses – ITS Standards Year 2 modules and additional courses.**
2. **Provide peer-to-peer assistance.**
3. **Provide T3 Webinars.**
4. **Offer half-day courses at professional meetings for Continuing Education Units.**
5. **Develop partnership for multimodal project.**
6. **Evaluate, update, and retire current courses.**

Outcomes:

- The ITS practitioner applies the knowledge, skills, and abilities gained from training to plan, design, deploy, operate, and maintain ITS applications.
- Users indicate that course offerings have met their learning objectives.
- New materials meet learning objectives outlined by PCB.
- Course materials are current and relevant to current or emerging ITS applications

Measures:	Target:
	• Complete assessment of a sample of agencies by 2014
• Assessment of KSAs in use on the job, 6 months after training	• 90 percent of PCB course attendees
• Percent of users who indicate that PCB courses, technical assistance, and workshops meet their learning objectives	• 100 percent by 2014
• Percent of new material covering learning objectives outlined by PCB	• 100 percent by 2012
• Percent of PCB course materials up-to-date and relevant	• 20 percent annual increase in number of new participants
• Expansion of the T3 webinar audience	
• Expansion of the Peer to Peer events	• 20 percent annual increase in number of new participants

Timeframe:

Short-term – Action 1

Intermediate-term – Action 4

Long-term – Actions 5-6

Ongoing – Actions 2-3

Objective 2.1: Develop a Network of Champions Who Promote the Value of ITS

Goal 2: Leadership Outreach

Background:

The PCB Program intends to engage decision makers by developing a network of ITS champions who will promote the use of ITS technologies based upon their experience. The PCB Program will identify and document the work of successful ITS implementation. Next, the executive sponsors of these ITS projects will be invited to contribute their endorsements through diverse channels such as printed material, video, and speaking engagements. This work will be carried out in conjunction with the ITS JPO Outreach and Communications Program.

Actions:

1. **Develop strategy for engaging high level decision makers. Possible approaches to explore include:**
   a. **Meetings and retreats**
   b. **Mentoring and coaching**
   c. **Peer-to-peer exchanges**

2. Implement strategy for engaging high level decision makers

Outcomes:

- Decision makers are motivated to implement proven ITS technologies and are aware of emerging research results.
- Consensus about the role of ITS champions in promoting ITS and the best way to engage high level decision makers.

Measures:	Target:
• Number of ITS endorsements by local, state, and federal agencies	• 50 percent annual increase
• Assessment of influence of ITS champions on investment decisions	• Complete assessment of a sample of ITS champions by 2014

Timeframe:

Short-term – Action 1
Intermediate-term – Actions 2

Objective 2.2: Highlight Best Practices and Model Users

Goal 2: Leadership Outreach

Background:
The PCB Program will focus on synthesizing the known benefits and costs of deployed ITS technologies for decision makers and others. The Program will explore additional methods of sharing successful ITS implementations including a peer-to-peer network of model users, which can be used to build the capacity of future leaders.

Actions:
1. Create database of model users of ITS solutions.
2. Develop material describing benefits of ITS, synthesized for decision maker.

Outcomes:
- Expedited decision making process for implementing proven ITS solutions.
- Network of model users raises awareness of proven ITS solutions; synthesized material is used in making ITS investments.
- Network of model users created; material developed meets PCB identified learning objectives for this audience.

Measures:	Target:
• Number of model users participating in PCB network • Percent of synthesized benefit/cost material meeting learning objectives	• 50 percent annual increase • 100 percent of material by 2013

Timeframe:
Intermediate-term- Actions 1-2

Objective 3.1: Provide an ITS Learning Portal

Goal 3: Knowledge Exchange

Background:
The PCB Program will develop an integrated online presence that provides access to the full range of learning available to the ITS professional from ITS JPO and its partners at ITS America, the American Association of State Highway and Transportation Officials (AASHTO), Institute of Transportation Engineers (ITE), the Transportation Research Board (TRB), and universities.

Actions:
1. **Develop business case for One Stop Shop/Knowledge Portal.**
2. **Develop Strategy for One Stop Shop/Knowledge Portal.**
3. **Design and implement One Stop Shop/Knowledge Portal.**

Outcomes:
- ITS community makes decisions based on the most relevant and current information as provided by the ITS PCB program.
- More effective ITS deployments.

Measures:	Target:
• Number of website users • Number of user contributions to website • User survey of website content and additional needs	• 75 percent annual increase • 75 percent annual increase • 90 percent satisfaction

Timeframe:
Short-term – Action 1
Intermediate-term – Actions 2-3

Objective 3.2: Build a Knowledge -Sharing Network for Just-in-Time Learning among Practitioners

Goal 3: Knowledge Exchange

Background:
The PCB Program will create a knowledge-sharing network for industry practitioners, specialists, and subject matter experts to share their knowledge, experience, best practices, and lessons learned. In FY2011, the Program will explore options and determine the best technology platform to support knowledge exchange. In FY2012-13, the Program will implement a prototype knowledge-sharing network.

Actions:
1. Draft white paper of approaches for knowledge-sharing network.

2. Develop business case and project scope.

3. Document user requirements.

4. Evaluate technology options.

5. Implement prototype.

Outcomes:
- More effective ITS deployments based upon improved knowledge of ITS workforce.
- ITS practitioners contribute knowledge, experience, and best practices to knowledge-sharing network.

Measures:	Target:
• User rating of effectiveness of knowledge sharing network • Number of Knowledge Sharing Network users • Number of Knowledge Sharing Network entries	• 90 percent satisfaction • 1,000 users by 2014 • 10,000 entries by 2014

Timeframe:
Short-term – Action 1
Intermediate-term – Actions 2-5

Objective 3.3: Develop a Collaborative Environment of Learning Providers Who Share Their Expertise

Goal 3: Knowledge Exchange

Background:

The PCB Program will develop a collaborative environment of learning providers who are willing to communicate, share best practices, and coordinate their efforts to deliver a consistent curriculum in ITS technologies.

Actions:

1. **Conduct PCB National Workshop to identify participants among learning providers.**
2. Create learning collaborative charter.
3. Determine key features of learning collaborative virtual environment.
4. Document procedures for sharing and disseminating learning best practices.

Outcomes:

- ITS learning providers gain knowledge of emerging ITS topics and state-of-the-art learning techniques.

- ITS practitioners learn more relevant information using the most effective delivery mechanisms.

Measures:	Target:
• User rating of effectiveness of learning collaborative • Number and diversity of learning providers participating • Number of collaborative learning environment content entries • Acceptance of learning collaborative charter by members	• 90 percent satisfaction • 100 learning providers by 2014 • 1,000 users by 2014 • 100 percent of members by end of 2011

Timeframe:

Short-term – Actions 1-2
Intermediate-term – Action 3
Long-term – Action 4

Objective 4.1: Increase Awareness of Current Research through Pilots and Demonstrations that Allow Interactive Hands-on Learning

Goal 4: Technology Transfer

Background:
The PCB Program will provide exposure and build competence in specific ITS technologies through the use of the ITS test beds, pilots, and demonstrations. The PCB Program will use interactive approaches, such as video game simulations, to provide experiential learning in ITS technologies.

Actions:
1. **Research test bed usage.**
2. **Develop strategy and guidelines for test bed usage.**
3. Develop interactive tools based upon users' experience with ITS demonstrations and simulations.
4. Disseminate information to university researchers.

Outcomes:
- Accelerated application of ITS solutions in the field.

Measures:	Target:
• Number of ITS test beds, pilots, and demonstrations performed	• 5 test beds by 2014
• Number of participating agencies, or organizations in ITS test beds, pilots, and demonstrations	• 20 participating agencies by 2014

Timeframe:
Short-term – Actions 1-2
Intermediate-term – Action 3
Long-term – Action 4

Objective 4.2: Embed Training and Outreach into the Research and Development Process to Move ITS Innovation into the Market Faster

Goal 4: Technology Transfer

Background:
This PCB Program will identify and develop processes and procedures to accelerate ITS research into practice.

Actions:
1. Create set of recommendations for a template to identify target audiences of new technologies.
2. Develop approach to identify how outreach and professional capacity building can be integrated into the technology development, testing, and evaluation lifecycle.
3. Update of ITS standards and architecture courses to leverage technology transfer practices.

Outcomes:
- ITS professionals implement technology more expeditiously.

Measures:	Target:
• Percent of agencies that have participated in ITS PCB programs implementing new technologies	• 50 percent annual increase
• Percent decrease in time to implement new technologies	• 50 percent annual decrease
• Number of ITS standards and architecture courses covering technology transfer	• 100 percent by 2014
• Number of technology products introduced to the commercial market as a result of ITS test beds	• 5 commercial technologies by 2014

Timeframe:
Intermediate-term – Actions 1-3

Appendix B Stakeholder Engagement

The Program used a targeted approach to gathering input from the following ITS PCB Program stakeholders:

Program Users: ITS practitioners

Project-based managers, contractors, technicians, and decision makers who are able to identify learning needs, audiences, timing for learning, and how they find learning to be delivered most effectively.

External ITS learning delivery partners

External entities and organizations in the business of training, technology transfer, and knowledge management who may be interested in leveraging efforts and forming more strategic partnerships. Examples of external delivery partners are universities and professional associations.

Internal program partners

ITS program managers and modal partners who fall into two categories:

- Those in charge of research who will help define the audience for the new technologies and the requirements for a technology transfer process that enables successful adoption, and
- Those who have helped assess the Program's resources and effectiveness for over a decade and who can provide input on the core elements of vision, mission, goals, and objectives.

ITS PCB Program Strategic Visioning Session

A strategic vision session was held on July 7, 2010 in Washington, DC to discuss strategy and set the future direction of the PCB Program. During that session, the leaders of the Program and representatives from key stakeholder groups shared their vision for the ITS PCB, analyzed the current state of the Program and the challenges facing it, then agreed upon the key focus areas that will guide the Program to achieve the desired future state.

The results of this session were drafted into the vision, mission, and core values for the ITS PCB Program. A preliminary set of goals for the Program were drafted for further validation by user and stakeholder groups. The group agreed to serve as an advisory board for the Strategic Plan as it was developed.

User Workshops

In the summer and fall of 2010, the ITS PCB Program conducted three user workshops. The first was delivered in person in conjunction with ITS Safety Workshop in Northbrook, IL on July 21, 2010. The second and third were based upon the first workshop, and delivered through an interactive web meeting format. The workshops were multimodal, involving transit and highway participants from the public and private sectors, as well as representatives from colleges, universities, and professional associations.

The workshops were designed to:

- Provide information about the current state and future direction of the ITS PCB Program.
- Identify learning needs.
- Determine preferred learning delivery mechanisms.
- Collect feedback on draft goals for the ITS PCB Program.

Workshop Results

Participants from the July 21 workshop voted for the ITS PCB Program goals that best met the criteria, "if this goal were achieved it would really help me perform my ITS work." The goals selected during that workshop were used to obtain additional feedback during the interactive web meetings.

One hundred forty-eight people participated in two interactive web meetings. Four poll questions focused on participant experiences regarding, 1) the types of ITS information needed, 2) the best ways to receive learning, 3) how to determine if a learning experience had value, and 4) needs for the advancement of their ITS career. The last question asked participants to rate their top five ITS PCB Program goals from a list previously developed by a group of core ITS PCB Program users and learning providers that participated in previous workshops. The participant feedback from the meetings is provided below.

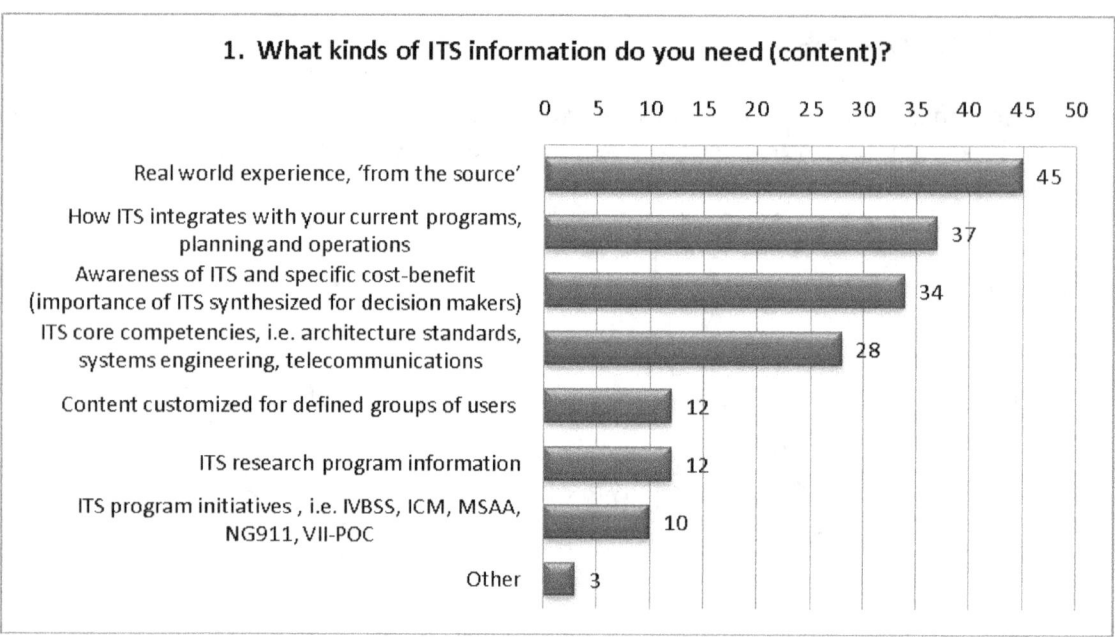

Figure B-1. Question 1 Results – What kinds of ITS information do you need?

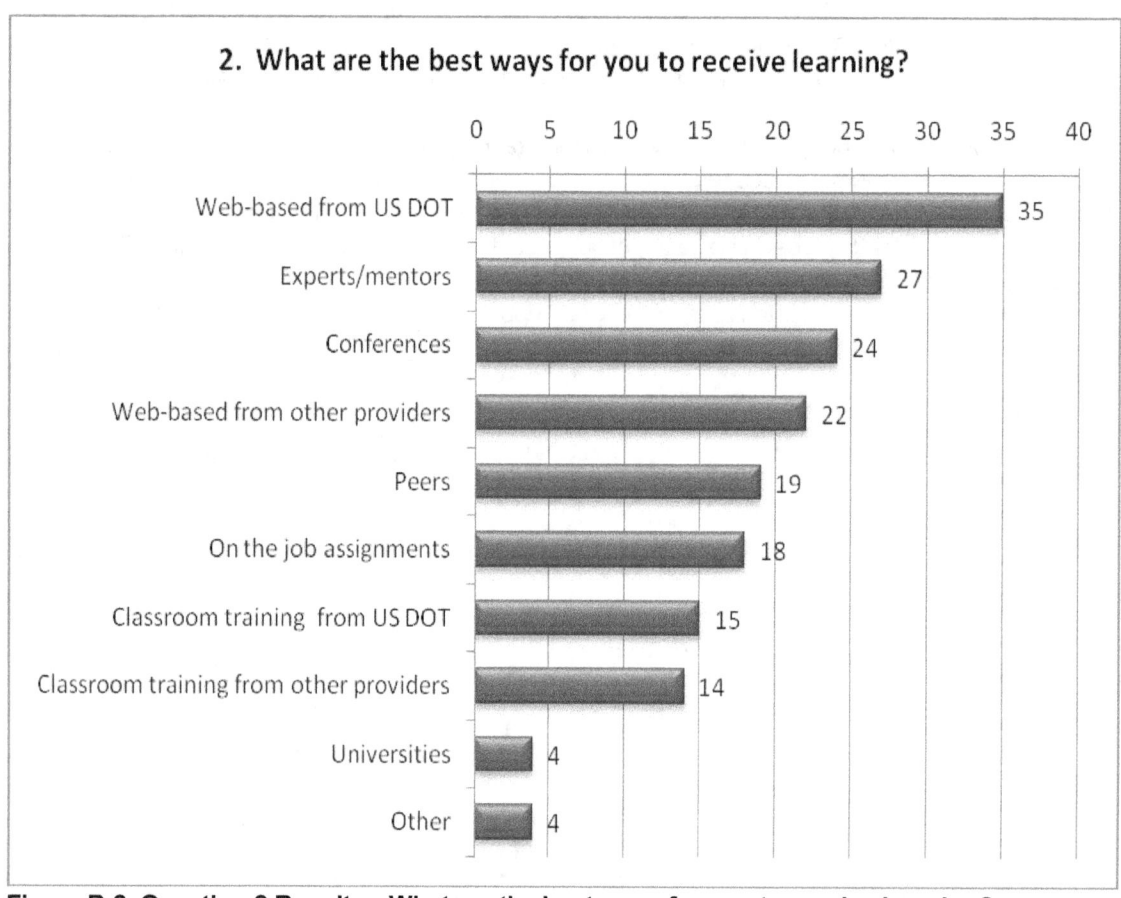

Figure B-2. Question 2 Results – What are the best ways for you to receive learning?

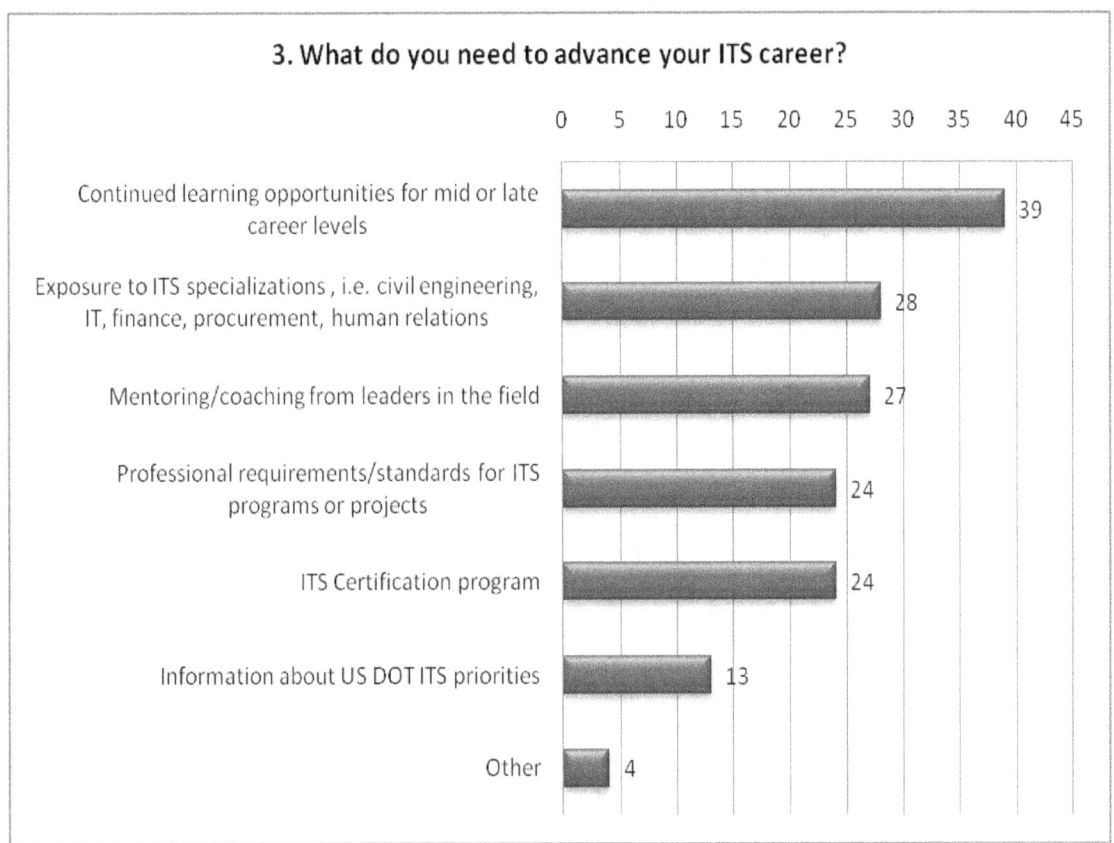

Figure B-3. Question 3 Results – What do you need to advance your ITS career?

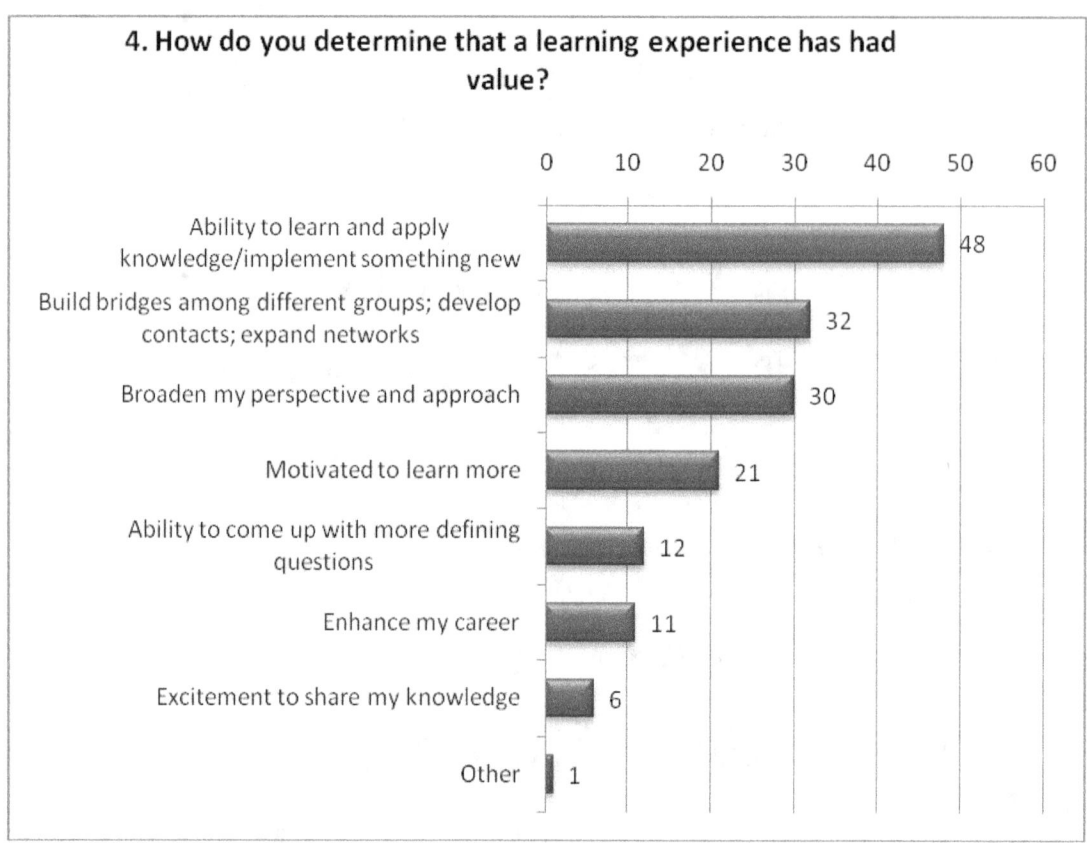

Figure B-4. Question 4 Results – How do you determine that a learning experience has had value?

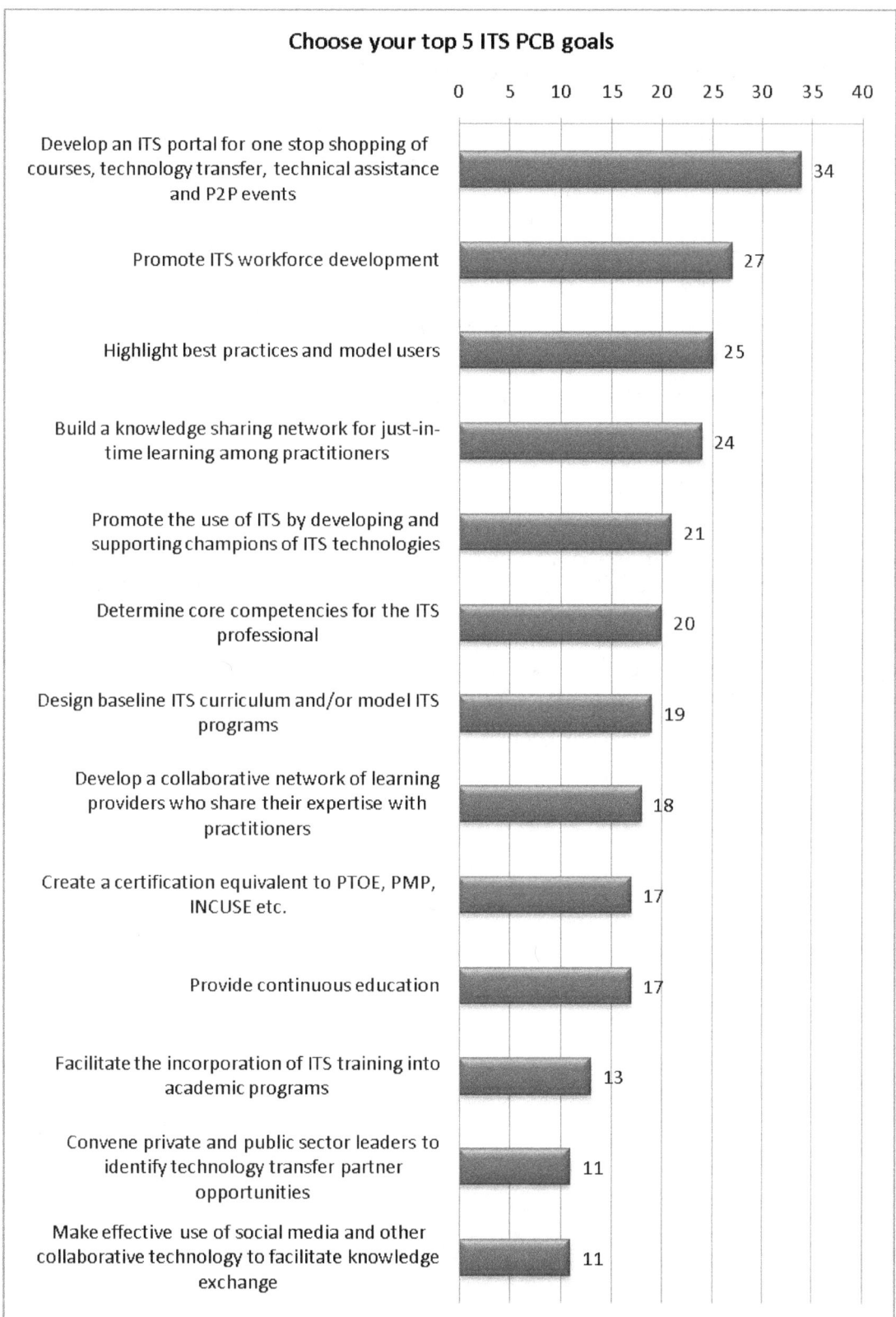

Figure B-5. Question 5 Results – Top ITS PCB Program Goals

University and Learning Provider Workshop

The fourth workshop was an interactive web meeting with university and learning provider participants held on November 17, 2010. The focus of this webinar was on innovative ways to partner with these organizations to deliver learning.

The workshop was designed to:

- Provide information about the current state and future direction of the ITS PCB program.
- Learn about what ITS topics are currently or will be offered by learning providers.
- Understand how institutions can partner with the ITS PCB Program.
- Collect feedback on draft goals for the ITS PCB Program.

Workshop Results

Forty people participated in the interactive web meeting. Four poll questions focused on participant experiences regarding, 1) the resources needed to expand ITS learning, 2) how to partner with the U.S. DOT to deliver ITS training, 3) how technology transfer is encouraged by the participants' organizations, and 4) how universities and other learning providers contribute to the development of the ITS workforce. The last question asked participants to rate their priority goals for the ITS PCB Program from a list of potential priorities previously developed by a group of core ITS PCB stakeholders. The participant feedback from the meetings is provided below.

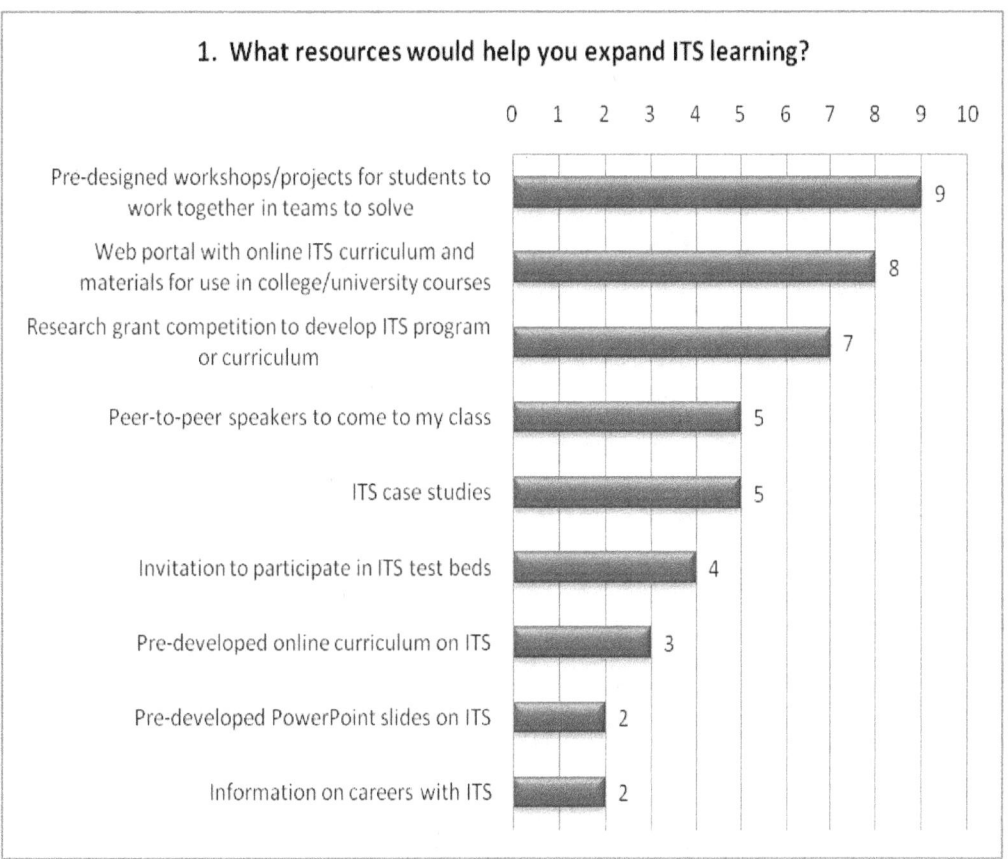

Figure B-6. Question 1 Results – What resources would help you expand ITS learning?

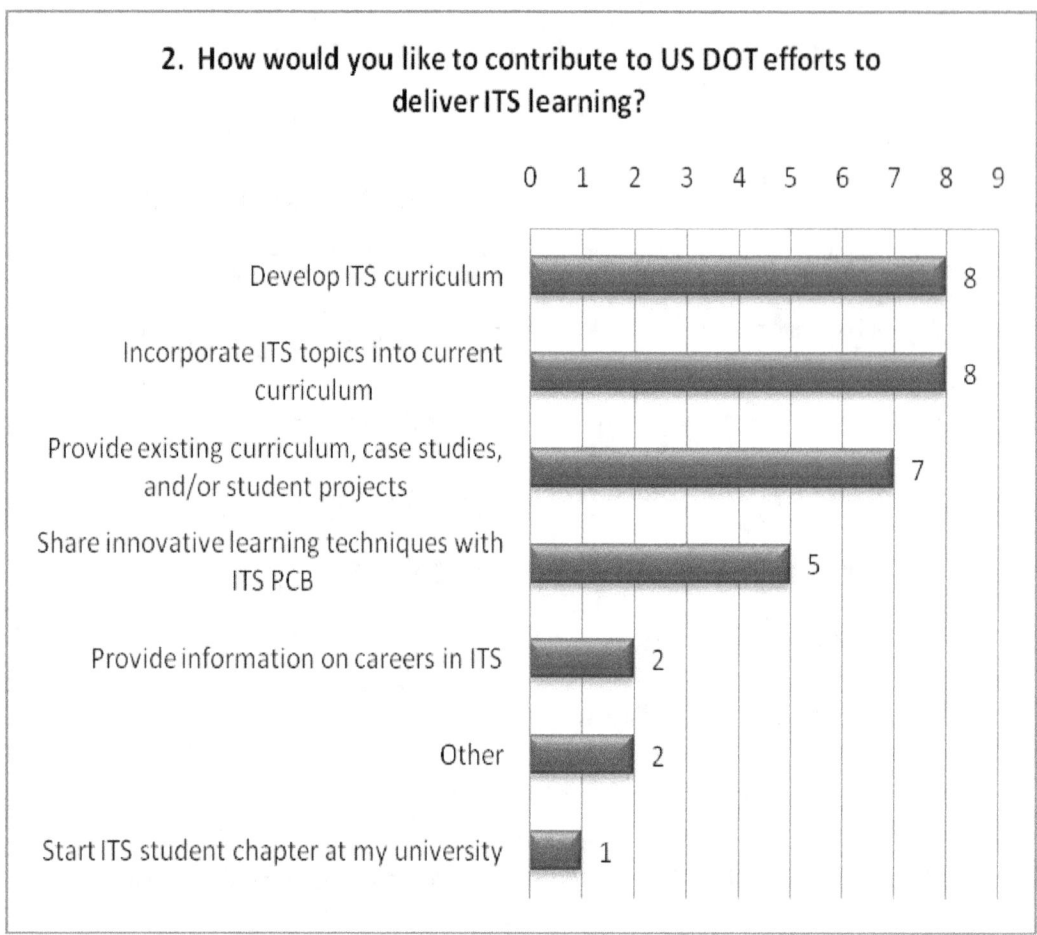

Figure B-7. Question 2 Results – How would you like to contribute to U.S. DOT efforts to deliver ITS learning?

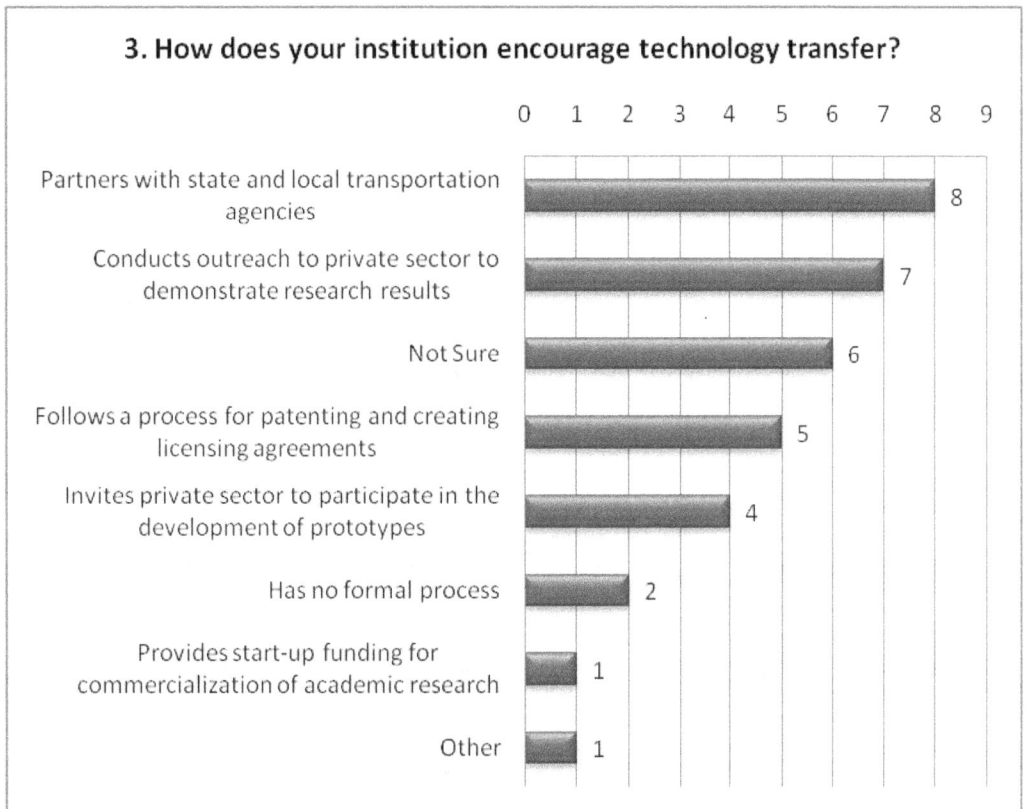

Figure B-8. Question 3 Results – How does your institution encourage technology transfer?

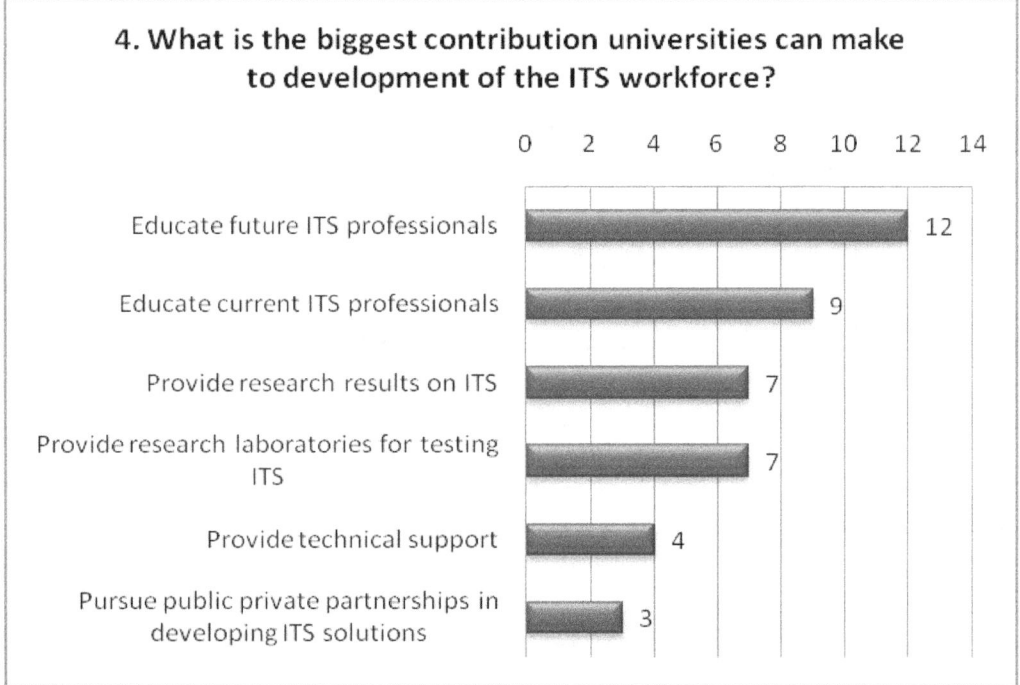

Figure B-9. Question 4 – What is the biggest contribution universities can make to the development of the ITS workforce?

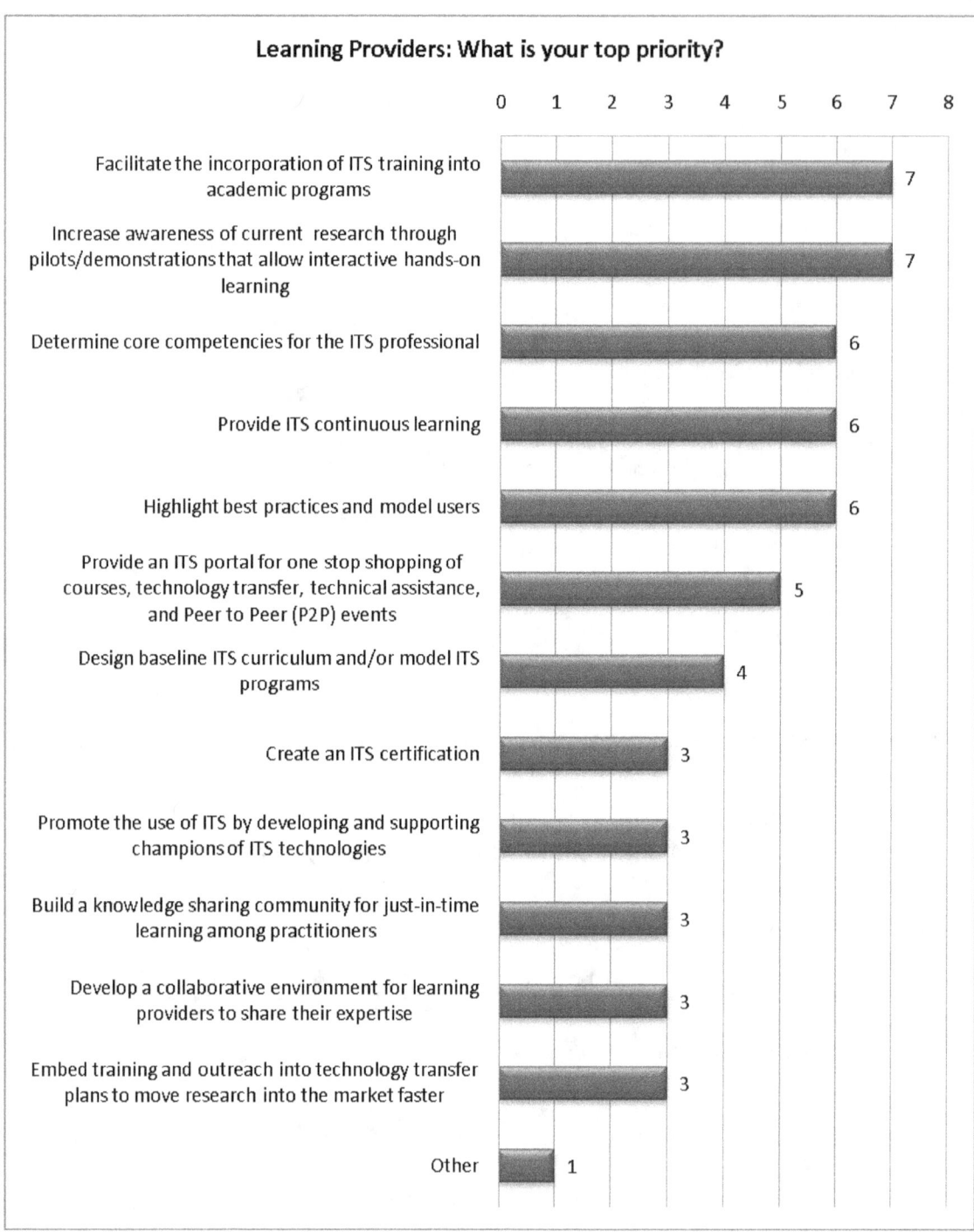

Learning Providers: What is your top priority?

Priority	Value
Facilitate the incorporation of ITS training into academic programs	7
Increase awareness of current research through pilots/demonstrations that allow interactive hands-on learning	7
Determine core competencies for the ITS professional	6
Provide ITS continuous learning	6
Highlight best practices and model users	6
Provide an ITS portal for one stop shopping of courses, technology transfer, technical assistance, and Peer to Peer (P2P) events	5
Design baseline ITS curriculum and/or model ITS programs	4
Create an ITS certification	3
Promote the use of ITS by developing and supporting champions of ITS technologies	3
Build a knowledge sharing community for just-in-time learning among practitioners	3
Develop a collaborative environment for learning providers to share their expertise	3
Embed training and outreach into technology transfer plans to move research into the market faster	3
Other	1

Figure B-10. Question 5 Results – Top ITS PCB Program Goals

U.S. Department of Transportation
ITS Joint Program Office-HOIT
1200 New Jersey Avenue, SE
Washington, DC 20590

Toll-Free "Help Line" 866-367-7487
www.its.dot.gov

[FHWA-JPO-11-078]

U.S. Department of Transportation

Research and Innovative Technology Administration